CLASSICAL *PIANO* SOLOS COLLECTION

VOLUME *TWO*

Agitato e con fuoco from Songs Without Words Felix Mendelssohn-Bartholdy **44**
Bydło from Pictures At An Exhibition Modeste Mussorgsky **28**
Chanson De Matin, Op.15, No.2 Edward Elgar **18**
Ecossaise Franz Schubert **38**
Gavotte from English Suite in G Minor Johann Sebastian Bach **6**
Good Morning Op.18, No.1 Eugene Goossens **22**
Humoreske from 5 Piano Pieces, Op.3 Carl Nielsen **30**
Jesu, Joy Of Man's Desiring Johann Sebastian Bach **8**
Kontre-Tänze No.1 Ludwig van Beethoven **12**
Mazurka, Op.101b Lennox Berkeley **16**
Musette en Rondeau Jean-Philippe Rameau **34**
Pleasing Landscape from Forest Scenes, Op.82 Robert Schumann **42**
Rococo Selim Palmgren **32**
Sonata K.353; L.313 Domenico Scarlatti **36**
The Entertainer Scott Joplin **24**
Valse Lente from Coppélia Léo Delibes **3**

Wise Publications
London/New York/Paris/Sydney/Copenhagen/Madrid

Exclusive Distributors:

Music Sales Limited
8/9 Frith Street, London W1V 5TZ, England.

Music Sales Pty Limited
120 Rothschild Avenue, Rosebery, NSW 2018, Australia.

Music Sales Corporation
257 Park Avenue South, New York, NY10010, United States of America.

Order No. AM91535
ISBN 0-7119-3757-5
This book © Copyright 1994 by Wise Publications

*Unauthorised reproduction of any part of this publication by
any means including photocopying is an infringement of Copyright.*

*Book design by Studio Twenty, London
Computer management by Adam Hay Editorial Design
Compiled by Stephen Duro*

*Printed in the United Kingdom by
J.B. Offset Printers (Marks Tey) Limited, Marks Tey, Essex.*

YOUR GUARANTEE OF QUALITY
As publishers, we strive to produce every book to the highest commercial standards.
This book has been carefully designed to minimise awkward page turns and to make
playing from it a real pleasure.
Particular care has been given to specifying acid-free, neutral-sized paper made from pulps
which have not been elemental chlorine bleached. This pulp is from farmed sustainable forests
and was produced with special regard for the environment.
Throughout, the printing and binding have been planned to ensure a sturdy,
attractive publication which should give years of enjoyment.
If your copy fails to meet our high standards, please inform us and
we will gladly replace it.

Music Sales' complete catalogue describes thousands of titles and
is available in full colour sections by subject, direct from Music Sales Limited.
Please state your areas of interest and send a cheque/postal order for £1.50 for postage to:
Music Sales Limited, Newmarket Road, Bury St. Edmunds, Suffolk IP33 3YB.

Valse Lente
from Coppélia
Composed by Léo Delibes

© Copyright 1994 Dorsey Brothers Music Limited, 8/9 Frith Street, London W1V 5TZ.
All Rights Reserved. International Copyright Secured.

Gavotte
from English Suite in G Minor
Composed by Johann Sebastian Bach

© Copyright 1994 Dorsey Brothers Music Limited, 8/9 Frith Street, London W1V 5TZ.
All Rights Reserved. International Copyright Secured.

GAVOTTE I (alternativamente)

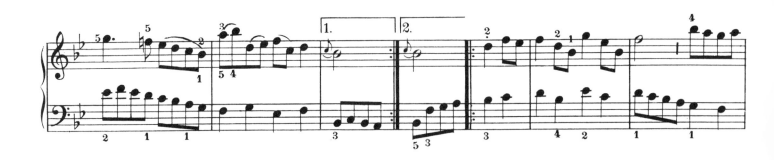

GAVOTTE II (ou la Musette)

Gavotte I da capo.

Jesu, Joy Of Man's Desiring

Composed by Johann Sebastian Bach

© Copyright 1994 Dorsey Brothers Music Limited, 8/9 Frith Street, London W1V 5TZ.
All Rights Reserved. International Copyright Secured.

Kontre-Tänze No.1

Composed by Ludwig Van Beethoven

© Copyright 1994 Dorsey Brothers Music Limited, 8/9 Frith Street, London W1V 5TZ.
All Rights Reserved. International Copyright Secured.

Mazurka
Op.101b

Composed by Lennox Berkeley

© Copyright 1994 Dorsey Brothers Music Limited, 8/9 Frith Street, London W1V 5TZ.
All Rights Reserved. International Copyright Secured.

Chanson De Matin
Op.15, No.2

Composed by Edward Elgar

© Copyright 1994 Dorsey Brothers Music Limited, 8/9 Frith Street, London W1V 5TZ.
All Rights Reserved. International Copyright Secured.

Good Morning
Op.18, No.1

Composed by Eugene Goossens

© Copyright 1994 Dorsey Brothers Music Limited, 8/9 Frith Street, London W1V 5TZ.
All Rights Reserved. International Copyright Secured.

The Entertainer
Composed by Scott Joplin

© Copyright 1994 Dorsey Brothers Music Limited, 8/9 Frith Street, London W1V 5TZ.
All Rights Reserved. International Copyright Secured.

Bydło
from Pictures At An Exhibition
Composed by Modeste Mussorgsky

© Copyright 1994 Dorsey Brothers Music Limited, 8/9 Frith Street, London W1V 5TZ.
All Rights Reserved. International Copyright Secured.

Humoreske
from 5 Piano Pieces, Op.3

Composed by Carl Nielsen

© Copyright 1994 Dorsey Brothers Music Limited, 8/9 Frith Street, London W1V 5TZ.
All Rights Reserved. International Copyright Secured.

Rococo

Composed by Selim Palmgren

© Copyright 1994 Dorsey Brothers Music Limited, 8/9 Frith Street, London W1V 5TZ.
All Rights Reserved. International Copyright Secured.

Musette en Rondeau

Composed by Jean-Philippe Rameau

© Copyright 1994 Dorsey Brothers Music Limited, 8/9 Frith Street, London W1V 5TZ.
All Rights Reserved. International Copyright Secured.

Sonata
K.353; L.313

Composed by Domenico Scarlatti

© Copyright 1994 Dorsey Brothers Music Limited, 8/9 Frith Street, London W1V 5TZ.
All Rights Reserved. International Copyright Secured.

Ecossaise

Composed by Franz Schubert

© Copyright 1994 Dorsey Brothers Music Limited, 8/9 Frith Street, London W1V 5TZ.
All Rights Reserved. International Copyright Secured.

Pleasing Landscape
from Forest Scenes, Op.82
Composed by Robert Schumann

Agitato e con fuoco
from Songs Without Words
Composed by Felix Mendelssohn-Bartholdy

© Copyright 1994 Dorsey Brothers Music Limited, 8/9 Frith Street, London W1V 5TZ.
All Rights Reserved. International Copyright Secured.